Schaum
Making Music Method

By John W. Schaum
Revised and Edited by Wesley Schaum

Level Two

T0078747

FOREWORD

The Schaum *Making Music Method* uses the proven middle-C approach integrated with ear, eye and finger training. This edition is the product of many years of teaching experience and continuing evaluation. Many careful refinements enhance the original pedagogic concepts.

Note reading proficiency is promoted by an emphasis on *training the eyes* to tecognize various melodic and harmonic intervals, up and down. The student is introduced to rudimentary *form and analysis* by learning to identify and recognize various melodic patterns and rhythmic patterns, indicated by a slur.

Self-help is encouraged by the inclusion of *Reference Pages* and a *Music Dictionary* in the book. The student can sound out pronunciations of musical terms by using the phonetic syllables provided.

The majority of music is *original*, composed by John W. Schaum. There are also transcriptions of folk songs and themes from master composers.

> The Schaum *Making Music Method* consists of *six books*, from Primer Level through Level 5

NOTE TO PARENTS

Regular practice is essential to progress at the piano. Assist your child by setting a consistent time for practice each day (except weekends and holidays). If practice is missed on a weekday, it could be made up during the weekend.

Quality of practice is more important than quantity. Try to structure household events to avoid interruptions and distractions during practice time. When practice is careful and attentive, 15 to 25 minutes per day is sufficient at this level.

Schaum Publications, Inc.

EXCLUSIVELY DISTRIBUTED BY

HAL•LEONARD®
CORPORATION
7777 W. BLUEMOUND RD. P.O. BOX 13819 MILWAUKEE, WI 53213

2

CONTENTS

Schaum's Curriculum for Musicianship Development

Student musicianship is developed by a balanced curriculum that includes:
- Note Reading and Music Theory
- Finger Strength and Dexterity
- Music Appreciation and Repertoire Development
- Rhythmic Training and Ensemble Experience

For Level Two supplements, books and sheet music, see our website
www.schaumpiano.net

Schaum Flash Cards – Intervals and Leger Lines

These flash cards contain a mixture of intervals, 2nds, 3rds, 4ths, 5ths and 6ths using leger lines above, between and below the treble and bass staffs. *Answers are printed on the back side.*

Recommendations for use:
• Identify the *interval number* by saying, "6th, 5th, 2nd, etc."
• Identify the *notes* by saying, "E and C, F and A, etc."
• Play the notes for each interval.

• Flash cards should be *reviewed* frequently.

• To encourage speed, the student may be timed with a watch. Keep track of the time and date in a notebook.

• May also be *used at home* with help from parents.

Preparation and storage (optional):
1. The flash cards may be made more durable by covering the entire page with *clear contact paper*, both front and back. 2. Cut apart on the dotted lines.
3. After cutting, keep the flash cards in an *envelope* taped to the back inside cover of this book.

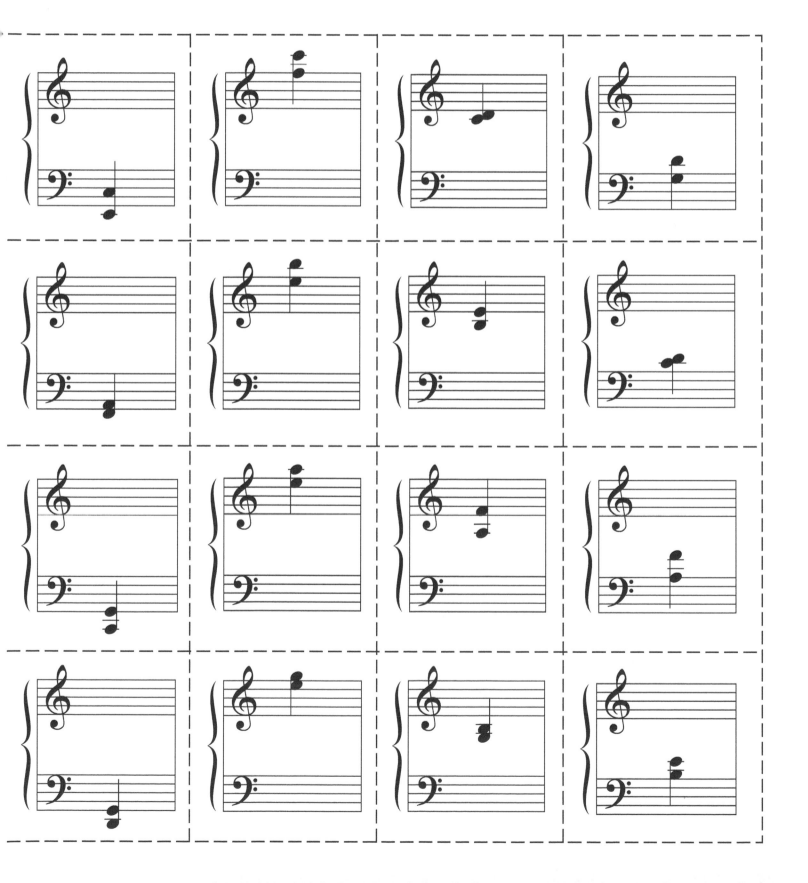

The answers are printed on the back of each flash card for the convenience of parents and teacher

Interval = 5th	Interval = 2nd	Interval = 5th	Interval = 6th
Bass Clef Notes:	Treble Clef Notes:	Treble Clef Notes:	Bass Clef Notes:
D	D	C	C
G	C	F	E

Interval = 2nd	Interval = 4th	Interval = 5th	Interval = 3rd
Bass Clef Notes:	Treble Clef Notes:	Treble Clef Notes:	Bass Clef Notes:
D	E	B	A
C	B	E	F

Interval = 6th	Interval = 6th	Interval = 4th	Interval = 5th
Bass Clef Notes:	Treble Clef Notes:	Treble Clef Notes:	Bass Clef Notes:
F	F	A	G
A	A	E	C

Interval = 4th	Interval = 3rd	Interval = 3rd	Interval = 4th
Bass Clef Notes:	Treble Clef Notes:	Treble Clef Notes:	Bass Clef Notes:
E	B	G	G
B	G	E	D

Rhythmland Express

DIRECTIONS: The music begins slowly, gets faster, then slows down as the train reaches the station. (See Music Dictionary on page 46.)

6

The **polka** is a lively, hopping dance still popular with many ethnic groups in Europe and the United States. A legend says it was invented about 1830 by a house servant in a village near Prague, Czech Republic. Because the room where she danced was small, she had to take short steps. The dance, therefore was named *polka* (meaning "half" or "short").

Penguin Polka

Vivace

It's pol - ka time in Pen - guin Town. They're com - ing in from all a - round. They're

all dressed up in for - mal wear. They look real deb - o - nair. They

strut and step, They swing and sway, They're full of kick, And ver - y chic. They're

poco a poco cresc.

all dressed up in for - mal wear. They look real deb - o - nair.

Frederic Chopin (SHOW-pan) was one of the greatest composers for the piano (1810-1849). He was born in Poland, but spent most of his last 17 years living in Paris, France, where he taught piano for a living.

A **mazurka** is a folk dance which originated in Warsaw, Poland. It is performed in 3/4 time, a little slower than waltz time. Chopin wrote more than fifty mazurkas.

Warsaw Mazurka

Moderato

Chopin, Op. 7, No. 3

The tempo mark at the beginning of this piece includes a **metronome mark**:

Allegretto ♩ = 126-144

The metronome mark has a note, an equals sign and one or two numbers. The numbers indicate **beats per minute**. For example, a metronome set at 60 will make 60 clicks per minute. The quarter note shown here gets one metronome click and usually, but not always, one count in the time signature.

In this piece, the two numbers in the metronome mark, 126-144, mean that the recommended *performance speed* is any tempo from 126 to 144. When practicing, your tempo may need to be slower than 126. Read more about the metronome and its use at the bottom of page 9.

Carousel Waltz

Allegretto ♩ = 126-144

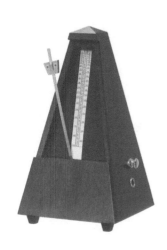

USE of the METRONOME

Metronome marks often include the letters **M.M.** This is an abbreviation of "Maelzel's Metronome." Maelzel was one of the early developers of the pyramid-shaped mechanical metronome. Modern metronomes are made in many shapes and sizes and may be electronic or mechanical.

Metronome speeds for various tempo markings are flexible. The master composers often did not agree. For example, Beethoven's Allegro was 88 and Mendelssohn's Allegro was 100. Recordings of the same piece performed by different concert pianists or different orchestral conductors also show considerable differences in tempo.

The metronome is primarily used briefly to set the tempo. It is not meant to be used all through a piece. Although practice with a metronome can be helpful in some situations, it is better to learn to play without constant use. The important thing is to maintain a steady, even beat.

New Key Signature: A Major

The three sharps used in the key signature for A major mean that **_all F's, C's and G's are sharp_**. The key signature eliminates the need to write a sharp sign for every F, C and G in the piece.

Windjammer

Allegro ♩ = 126-144

*Sea Chanty

Then blow ye winds, hi-ho! A-rov-ing I will go! I'll stay no more up-on the shore, So let the mu-sic play! I'll cross the rag-ing *main! I'll fight the hur-ri-cane! For it's at sea I love to be, Ten thou-sand miles a-way!

* A *windjammer* is a large ocean going sailing ship. A *sea chanty* is a song sung by sailors in rhythm with their work. *Raging main* is a stormy ocean.

Accompaniment (stem up = R.H. stem down = L.H.)

Finger Workout
Play this exercise five times daily as a warm-up for "The Mailman."

The Mailman

Moderato ♩ = 112-120

Here's Stan - ley, our mail-man, With his bun - dles of mail. He comes with his mail bag, Be it sun, rain, or hail. Bring-ing let-ters, Bring-ing post cards, Mag-a -zines and oth-er mail. That's Stan - ley, our mail-man, Chil-dren fol - low his trail.

Damper Pedal

The damper pedal of a piano is the one farthest to the right. It is used to <u>blend sounds, to help connect notes smoothly and to enhance the sound</u> of the instrument.

The damper pedal is pressed with the toe of your right foot. Your **heel should always be on the floor**. When using the pedal, be sure to *lift it all the way up*, but without lifting your heel. Don't use the pedal as a footrest as you play, otherwise there will be a continuous blurred sound.

Movement of the pedal should be **silent**. Your foot should keep in contact with the pedal as it is used. Be careful not to let the pedal clunk or thump on the way down or up. If the pedal squeaks or makes a clicking noise, it should be repaired by a qualified technician.

Marking for the damper pedal looks like a bracket, printed below the lower staff.
The vertical line at each end indicates down and up, as shown below.

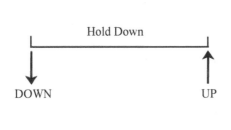

• When the pedal mark moves **down**,
the pedal is to be *pressed down with the right foot*.

• The **horizontal line** of the pedal mark
indicates that the pedal is to *remain pressed down*.

• When the pedal mark goes **up**,
the pedal is to be lifted silently, all the way up.
The heel must remain on the floor.

The *vertical lines* at the beginning and end of a pedal mark are important. In the warmup below, notice that each vertical line is printed *directly below a note* in the bass staff. Movement of the pedal down or up should be **at the same time as you play the note**.

For example, in the first measure of the pedal warm-up, the start of the pedal mark is directly below the first count of the measure. This means that you should press the pedal down as you play the note on the first count. The pedal is to remain down until the first beat of the next measure. Then lift the pedal at the same time as you play the note on the first count.

Pedal movement up or down may occur on *any count* in any measure.

Pedal Warm-Up (Preparatory for page 13)

DIRECTIONS: This warm-up has the same pedal markings used in "The Drum Major." The arrows show pedal movement down and up. Be careful – your foot should move down or up at **exactly the same time as you play the note** on the first beat of each measure. Play this line 4 or 5 times each day.

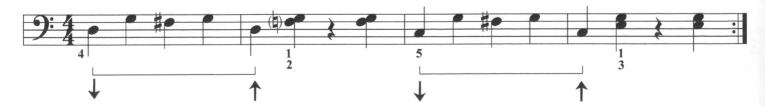

Teacher's Note: Use of the damper pedal to achieve a legato effect ("legato pedal" or "syncopated pedal") is purposely delayed until the student acquires more pedal experience and technical skill.

The Drum Major

Con vivo ♩ = 160-176

*von Suppé

Pedal mark continued from end of previous line of music.

* Franz von Suppé (soo-PAY) was an Austrian composer best known for his operettas (1819-1895).

Seeds Go Traveling

Moderato ♩ = 104-116

Au-tumn is the time, Seeds go trav-el-ing. They go man-y ways, Wa-ter, land, or air.

Some have ti-ny wings, Some hitch rides on clothes. Some hitch rides on fur, Seeds go ev-'ry-where.

All the trees have seeds, Flow-ers too have seeds. E-ven weeds have seeds, All float in the breeze.

Seeds go ev-'ry-where, Wa-ter, land, or air. Au-tumn is the time, Seeds go trav-el-ing.

Teacher's Note: Although this piece is in the key of E minor, F# has intentionally been omitted in the key signature. Minor tonalities will be presented later in this series.

Rhythm Section (Preparatory)

4   1 2 3 + 4 +   1 2 3 4   1 2 3 + 4 +   1 2 3 4

Count out loud and clap on each note.
The plus sign (+) is the abbreviation for "and."

Shops of Olden Times

Andantino

= 92–104

The shops of old-en times, Were not the su-per kind. The

prod - ucts that were sold seem ver-y old as we look back.

Yet folks got a - long, Al - though we won-der how. Who

knows what will come next, A hun-dred years from to - day!

Teacher's Note: The left hand melody uses **chromatic** movement, up and down (made up entirely of half steps).

Dotted Quarter Note and Single 8th Note

A single 8th note has a curved line attached to its stem. The curved line is called a *flag*. The flag is always placed *on the right side of the stem*. See the samples to the right.

A dot placed to the right of a quarter note *increases the length* of that note by one half.

A quarter note plus a dot is the same length as a quarter note tied to an 8th note.

A dotted quarter note is often used with a single 8th note. The counting is shown in the first sample measure.

Notice that the rhythm is the same when a quarter note is tied to the first of a pair of 8th notes, as shown in the 2nd sample measure.

America

Teacher's Note: The student should say the word "and" where a plus sign (+) is written. Other abbreviations of "and" may be used, if desired. If necessary to help keep a steady beat, all beats may be subdivided with a plus sign. However, this method of counting should be used only as a remedial aid.

The right hand melody is grouped into two-measure phrases. Some of these phrases are the same. For example, in the 1st, 2nd and 4th lines of music, the *notes in the first phrase are the same in each line*.

The left hand accompaniment is made up of three different patterns. Each pattern is shown with a phrase mark.

Disc Jockey

Allegretto ♩ = 104-116

Count → 1 2 + 3 4 + 1 2 + 3 4

mf On the ra-dio ev-'ry day, Fav'-rite re-cords he will play.

Tell-ing time and temp-'ra-ture, And the weath-er too.

f In be-tween com-mer-cials come, News re-ports from 'round the world.

mf On the ra-dio ev-'ry day, He has lots to say.

18

Finger Workout   Play this exercise five times daily as a warm-up for "Bobbin' for Apples."

Bobbín' for Apples

8th note gets one count

Giocoso ♪ = 144-160

*Sullivan

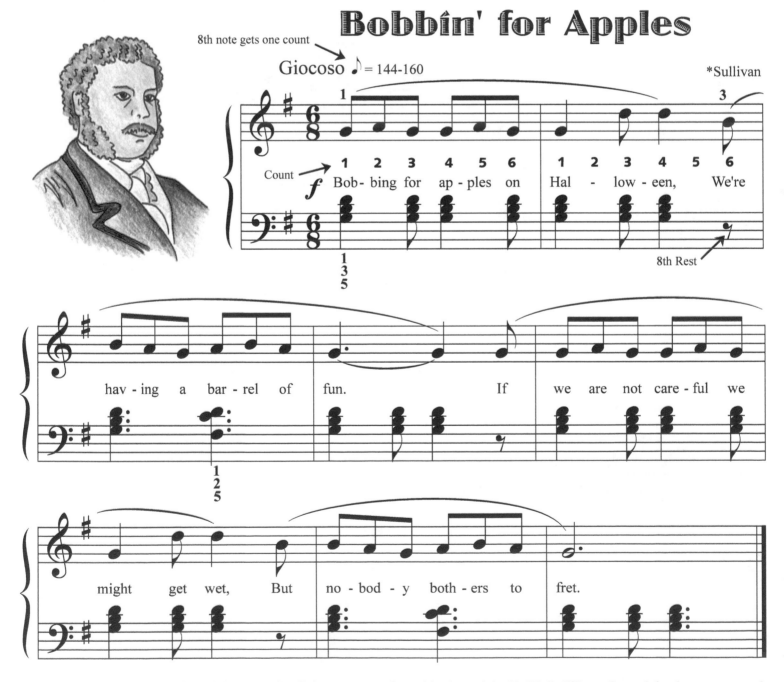

Count: 1 2 3 4 5 6 | 1 2 3 4 5 6
Bob- bing for ap-ples on Hal- low-een, We're

8th Rest

hav- ing a bar-rel of fun.   If we are not care-ful we

might get wet, But no-bod- y both-ers to fret.

* Sir Arthur Sullivan (1842-1900) was an English composer who, with playwright Sir W. S. Gilbert, formed the famous team of Gilbert & Sullivan. Together they wrote 18 operettas. This theme is from their operetta, *The Mikado*.

Sea Shell Serenade

Cantabile ♪ = 120-138

French Folk Tune

Count → 6 1 2 3 4 5 6 1 2 3 4 5 6

f I found a big brown sea shell. I held it to my

ear and heard, *p* A strange new kind of mu - sic. It

was the mu - sic of the sea, *f* A sea shell ser - e - nade.

Accompaniment (Double bar indicates end of each line in student part.)

Reminder: Look in the Music Dictionary on page 46 whenever you have a question about a musical term.

Paul Bunyan Legend

No one actually knows who invented the Paul Bunyan myth. His legendary exploits were related on winter evenings when old lumberjacks swapped exaggerated stories around the fireplace.

Paul Bunyan

Pesante ♩ = 116-126

Paul Bun - yan, the strong - est and big - gest of men, His height was as tall as a moun - tain. He chopped red - woods down with one blow of his ax, Then drank a whole lake full of wa - ter. He al - so did

farm - ing in such a big way, His corn crop grew tall - er than tim - ber. When men get to - geth - er and tall tales are told, The tall - est ones are of Paul Bun - yan!

Fermata* — a tempo*

* **Fermata** (𝄐) is a musical symbol meaning to **hold or pause** on a note for a short time. The note is held longer than its usual value. In this measure, the bass note is held while the treble note is played and held. Both notes are released at the same time. **A tempo** means to resume the previous tempo.

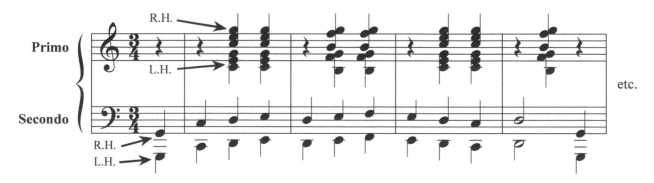

PAUL BUNYAN DUET – The **Primo** part (1st player) plays the *treble clef* part as written but *with the left hand*. The right hand plays the same treble clef notes *one octave higher than written*.

Primo
Secondo

R.H.
L.H.
etc.

The **Secondo** part (2nd player) plays the *bass clef* part as written but *with the right hand*. The left hand plays the same bass clef notes *one octave lower* than written.

22

The Ostrich

Vivace ♩ = 144-168

Tchaikowsky*, Op. 10, No. 2

* Peter Ilyich Tchaikowsky (chy-CUFF-skee) Russian composer most famous for his symphonies and ballets (1840-1893). The abbreviation **Op.** stands for *Opus* (OH-puss), meaning work or composition. An opus can be a short piece, a set of pieces, or an entire symphony. Op. 10 is a set of two piano pieces written in 1871. Tchaikowsky's last work is Op.79 (1893).

Finger Workout
Play this exercise five times daily as a warm-up for "Pony Express."

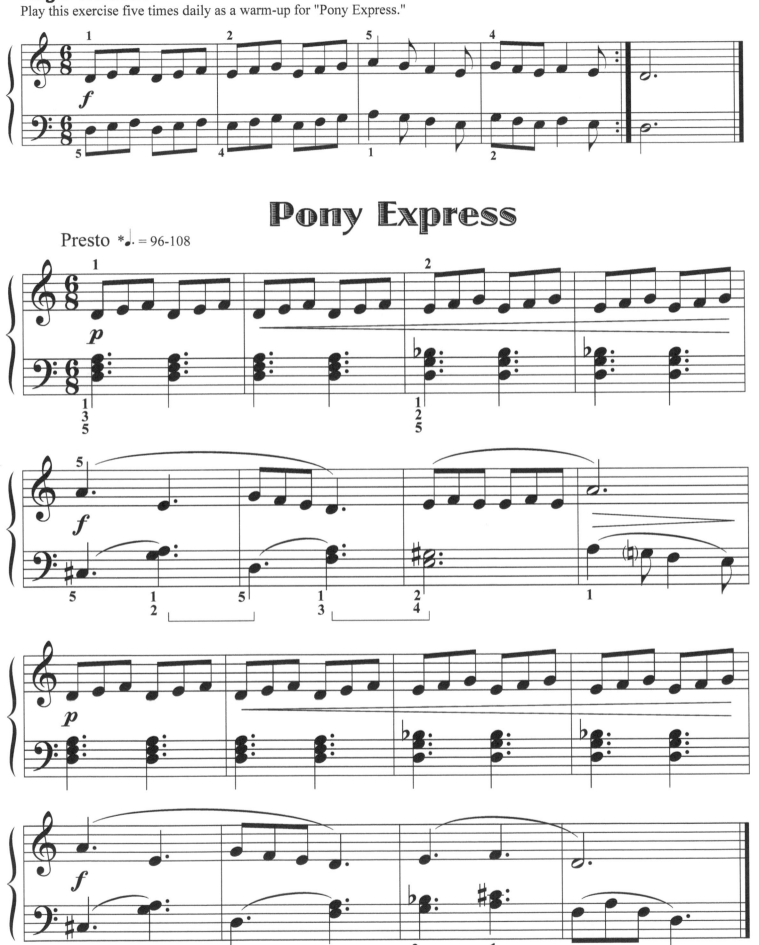

Pony Express

Presto *♩. = 96-108

* In this piece, each metronome "click" equals a ***dotted quarter note***. In fast 6/8 time, it is usually easier to think of two main counts in each measure, rather than all six counts. The two main counts are 1 and 4.

24

Patterns and Phrase Marks

Phrase marks help identify patterns in both melody and accompaniment. Many of these patterns are repeated. For example, the left hand pattern in the first measure is found in eight other measures. The left hand pattern in the 3rd measure is found in two other measures.

Recognizing patterns makes music reading and memorizing easier and faster.

Daylight Saving Time*

Moderato ♩ = 112-126

Set your clocks, Twice a year, Day - light Sav-ing Time.

Spring a - head, Fall be - hind, Day - light Sav-ing Time.

You will re - mem - ber it eas - y this way.

Spring a - head, Fall be - hind, Day - light Sav-ing Time!

* Each spring, many sections of the country go on Daylight Saving Time by setting the clocks *one hour ahead* (spring ahead). In the fall, the clocks are set *back one hour* (fall behind).

Making Music Quiz No. 1

DIRECTIONS: Match each musical term in the left column with the correct definition in the right column. Write the alphabetical letter of the definition on the proper line. For example, number **1** (*a tempo*) means <u>resume original tempo</u>; therefore the letter **k** has been placed on the line. If necessary, refer to the Reference Page (page 48) or the Music Dictionary (pages 46-47).

K 1. *a tempo*

____ 2. (key signature with three sharps)

____ 3. Tchaikowsky

____ 4. (6/8 time signature)

____ 5. Andante

____ 6. polka

____ 7. *poco a poco*

____ 8. ♩ = 126-144

____ 9. (bracket/tie symbol)

____ 10. Chopin

____ 11. *accel.*

____ 12. ♩. (dotted quarter note)

____ 13. mazurka

____ 14. F. von Suppé

____ 15. chromatic

____ 16. ⌢ (fermata symbol)

____ 17. ⁊ (eighth rest symbol)

____ 18. Arthur Sullivan

____ 19. opus

____ 20. chanty

A. fermata (pause)

B. Polish composer

C. damper pedal mark

D. progressing by half steps

E. key signature of A major

F. musical work or composition

G. six beats per measure

H. play faster

I. Austrian composer

J. Polish folk dance in 3/4 time

K. resume original tempo

L. moderately slow

M. English composer

N. song sung by sailors

O. little by little

P. metronome mark

Q. Russian composer

R. a lively hopping dance

S. ♩♪ (slurred notes symbol)

T. eighth rest

Teacher's Note: If desired, this quiz may be graded. Give 5 points for each correct answer.
A total score of 65 is passing – 70 is fair – 80 is good – 90 is very good – 95 or above is excellent.

New Key Signature: E♭ Major

The three flats used in the key signature for E♭ major mean that **all B's, E's and A's are flat**. The key signature eliminates the need to write a flat sign for every B, E and A in the piece.

The Old Oaken Bucket

Dolce ♩ = 108-116

George Kiallmark*

f The old oak-en buck - et, the i - ron clad buck - et, The *p* moss cov -ered buck - et that hung in the well. *f* How dear to my heart are the scenes of my child-hood, When *p* fond rec-ol -lec - tion pre -sents them to view.

* The melody of "The Old Oaken Bucket" is used for the *alma mater* song of Brown University in Providence, Rhode Island.

D.C. al fine is an abbreviation of the Italian phrase, *da capo al fine* (dah KAH-poh ahl FEE-nay). It means to <u>return to the beginning of the music and play to the word *fine*.</u>

Da capo means "from the beginning."
Fine means "end."

Cherry Blossom Festival

28

Mount Vernon Bells

Vessels and ships going up and down the Potomac River toll their bells when passing Mount Vernon as a tribute to the memory of George Washington.

Andante ♩ = 88-96

Stephen Foster*

* Stephen Foster (1826-1864) was the first great American song writer. The words in this piece were written by M.B.C. Slade and were added later to the music by Stephen Foster.

* **Coda** means *closing theme*. It is an extra group of measures added to the regular ending. Notice that the coda has exactly the same notes as the introduction (first four measures, page 28) except that the right hand part is written using leger lines.

Two Colonial Dances
1. Minuet

The *Minuet* (min-you-ETT) is a dignified dance for couples with a slow to moderate tempo in 3/4 time that was **very popular in George Washington's time**. The dance originated in France. The name *minuet* means small, referring to the steps of the dancers. Grieg wrote this piece in the style of the old-fashioned minuets.

Grazioso ♩ = 104-112

*Grieg, Op. 68, No. 2

* Edvard Grieg (GREEG) Norway's greatest composer (1843-1907).

2. Gavotte

The **Gavotte** (gah-VAHT) is also of French origin. It is livelier than the *minuet*. The *gavotte* was very popular during the 1600's and 1700's. It is usually written in 4/4 time.

Allegro ♩ = 138-160

Mozart*

* Wolfgang Amadeus Mozart (MOE-tsart) is one of the world's most famous composers. He was born in Austria (1756-1791).

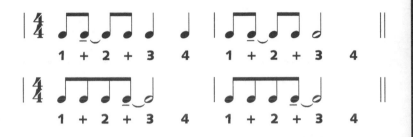

Syncopation is the emphasis of notes *between* the numbered counts, as shown by the accent mark (–) in the lines below. The plus sign (+) is the abbreviation for "and."

Indian Rain Dance

Spiritoso ♩ = 116-132

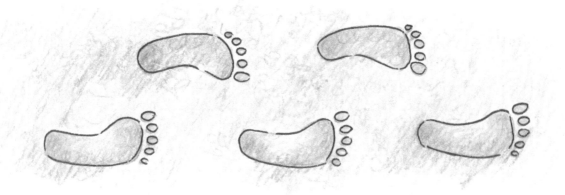

Footprints In the Sand

Giocoso ♪ = 132-152*

* Notice that the **8th note** is to be played at the metronome tempo indicated.

These lyrics were written by Anne Weston, age 11:
I was walking in the sand and watching all the seagulls land and
Tommy (he's my brother) helped me build a castle, it was grand; and
Then a pony came a-prancing and it looked like he was dancing.
Then we went home happy as a merry circus clown.

Listening for Major and Minor

Music expresses many moods. Music written in a **major** key usually has a cheerful and happy sound. Music written in a **minor** key often sounds sad, mysterious or spooky.

Here are two versions of "Yankee Doodle". The first is in the key of C *major*, the second is in the key of C *minor*. Listen carefully for the difference in sound.

Yankee Doodle (Key of *C major*)

Yankee Doodle (Key of *C minor*)*

* Teacher's Note: The purpose of these pieces is to demonstrate the *difference in sound* between major and minor. The key signature for C minor is purposely omitted here. The concept of relative major and minor, along with minor scales, will be taught later in this series.

34

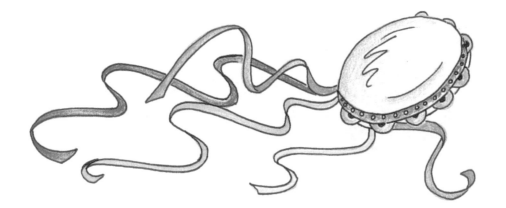

Gypsy Tambouríne*

Rameau*

Vivo ♩ = 126-144

* This piece is in the key of *A minor*. – Jean Philippe Rameau (rah-MOH) Early French composer (1683-1764).

Wedding March

Maestoso ♩ = 112-132

Wagner (VAHG-ner)*

* Richard Wagner is Germany's best known opera composer (1813-1888). The "Wedding March" is from his opera, *Lohengrin*.

Two Ways of Writing Notes for Left Hand

In the first two lines of music, left hand notes are written using *leger lines* in the bass staff.

In the last two lines, left hand notes in the lower staff are written in the *treble clef*.

Fireflies

Scherzando ♩ = 152-176

Fire - flies, fire - flies, in the night, Fire - flies, fire - flies, flick - 'ring lights.

Fire - flies, fire - flies, see them glow, Fire - flies, fire - flies, off they go.

Fire - flies, fire - flies, in the trees, Fire - flies, fire - flies, in the breeze.

Fire - flies, fire - flies, in the air, Fire - flies, fire - flies, ev - 'ry - where.

38

A *carillon* (CARE-reh-lahn) is a set of large bells on which melodies can be played. A church may have a bell tower with a carillon. The bell sounds are sometimes electronic.

The *Westminster Peal* is a famous 8-measure clock tower melody that originated in England. The same melody is often used in chiming clocks. The Westminster Peal is in the first two lines of music.

Carillon Tower

Semplice ♩ = 76-88

(Hold pedal down for this entire line.)

Time Signature Change

mf

D.C. al Fine

* The **interval of a 6th** is used for the melody throughout. Use right hand fingers 5 and 1 in all measures.

16th Notes

The stems of 16th notes are joined by TWO heavy lines called a *double beam*.

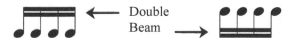 ← Double Beam →

A group of FOUR 16th notes fits into the same time space as ONE quarter note. Four 16th notes get one count.
The counting has extra syllables* because the beat is divided into more parts: **1 e + a**, **2 e + a**, and so on. See the counting printed between staffs in the music below.

Ghost Town

Misterioso ♩ = 126-144

* Teacher's Note: Syllables here are to be said "four - ee - and - ah." When the 16th notes occur on the 2nd beat, say "two - ee - and - ah."
Other ways of subdividing the beats are four syllable words such as "Mis-sis-sip-pi" or "Chat-ta-noo-ga."

40

16th Notes in 2/4 Time

TWO 16th notes fit into the same time space as ONE 8th note.

The counting has extra syllables as in 4/4 time (see page 39). Counting is printed between staffs in the music below.

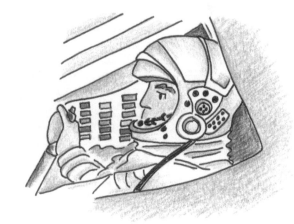

Test Pilot

Con brio ♩= 80-96

von Flotow*

* Friedrich von Flotow (FLOH-toh) was a German opera composer (1812-1883). This theme is taken from his opera, *Martha*.

3/8 Time Signature

3 – Three counts or beats in each measure
8 – 8th note gets One Count

♪ = 1 count   ♫ = 1 count   ♩ = 2 counts   ♩. = 3 counts

Notice that *two 16th notes get one count*. Samples of counting are
shown between staffs in the music below.

Put Your Little Foot

Vivace ♪ = 116-138

Traditional Folk Dance

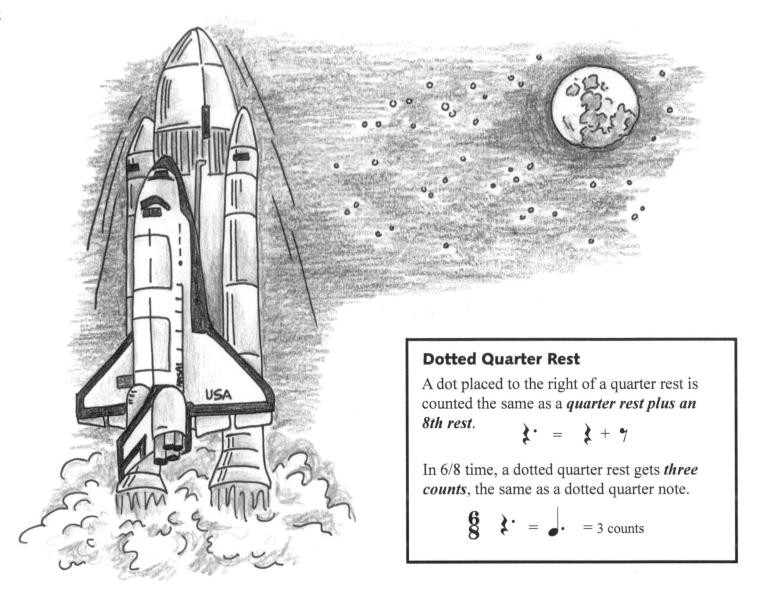

Dotted Quarter Rest

A dot placed to the right of a quarter rest is counted the same as a *quarter rest plus an 8th rest*.

$$\xi\cdot \;=\; \xi \;+\; \gamma$$

In 6/8 time, a dotted quarter rest gets *three counts*, the same as a dotted quarter note.

$$\frac{6}{8} \quad \xi\cdot \;=\; \downarrow\cdot \;=\; 3 \text{ counts}$$

Flight Of the Astronaut

Making Music Quiz No. 2

DIRECTIONS: Match each musical term in the left column with the correct definition in the right column. Write the alphabetical letter of the definition on the proper line. For example, number **1** (*leggiero*) means <u>lightly</u>; therefore the letter **m** has been placed on the line. If necessary, refer to the Reference Page (page 48) or the Music Dictionary (pages 46-47).

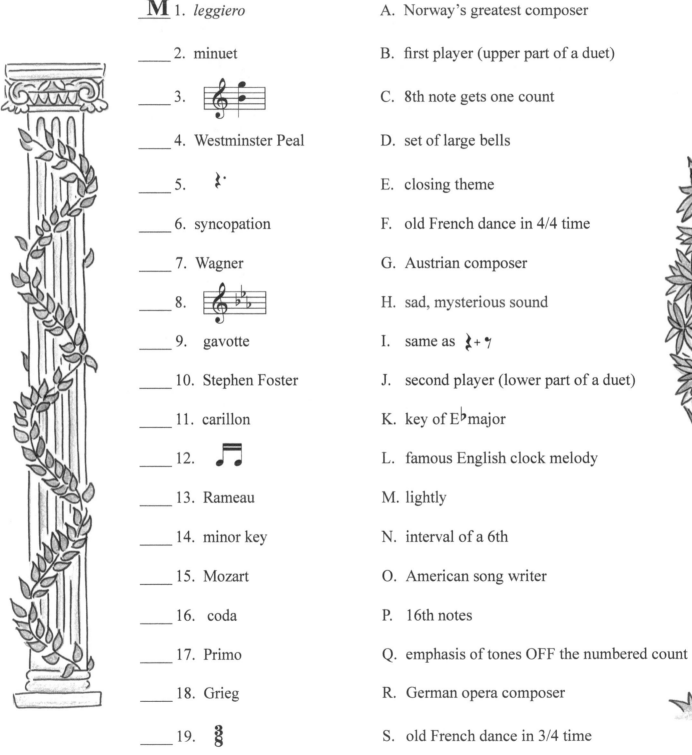

_M_ 1. *leggiero*

2. minuet

3.

4. Westminster Peal

5.

6. syncopation

7. Wagner

8.

9. gavotte

10. Stephen Foster

11. carillon

12.

13. Rameau

14. minor key

15. Mozart

16. coda

17. Primo

18. Grieg

19.

20. Secondo

A. Norway's greatest composer

B. first player (upper part of a duet)

C. 8th note gets one count

D. set of large bells

E. closing theme

F. old French dance in 4/4 time

G. Austrian composer

H. sad, mysterious sound

I. same as

J. second player (lower part of a duet)

K. key of E♭ major

L. famous English clock melody

M. lightly

N. interval of a 6th

O. American song writer

P. 16th notes

Q. emphasis of tones OFF the numbered count

R. German opera composer

S. old French dance in 3/4 time

T. early French composer

Teacher's Note: If desired, this quiz may be graded. Give 5 points for each correct answer.
A total score of 65 is passing – 70 is fair – 80 is good – 90 is very good – 95 or above is excellent.

Certificate
of Progress

This certifies that

_____

has successfully completed

LEVEL TWO

of the Schaum

Making Music Method

**and is eligible for advancement to
LEVEL THREE**

_____
Teacher

_____
Date

Reference Page and Music Dictionary – also see page 48

KEY SIGNATURES:

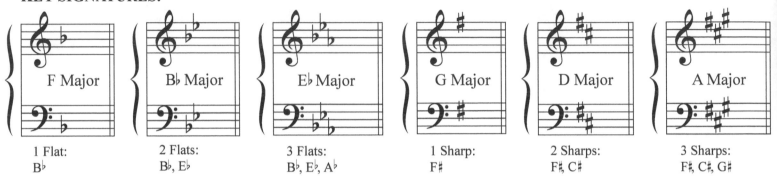

F Major	B♭ Major	E♭ Major	G Major	D Major	A Major
1 Flat: B♭	2 Flats: B♭, E♭	3 Flats: B♭, E♭, A♭	1 Sharp: F♯	2 Sharps: F♯, C♯	3 Sharps: F♯, C♯, G♯

MUSIC DICTIONARY

Terms listed here are limited to those commonly found in Level Two methods and supplements. Pronunciations have accented syllables shown in capital letters.

accel. = **accelerando** (ahk-sell-er-ON-doh) Becoming gradually faster in tempo.

accent (ACK-sent) Stress or emphasis on a note or chord.

accent marks: – > ᴧ

accidental (ack-sih-DEN-tal) Sharp, flat or natural that does *not* appear in the key signature. An accidental in parenthesis is a *reminder accidental.*

adagio (ah-DAH-jee-oh) Slow, slowly.

agitato (ahd-jih-TAH-toh) Agitated, restless.

allegretto (ah-leh-GRET-toh) A little slower than *allegro.*

allegro (ah-LEH-grow) Fast, quickly.

andante (ahn-DAHN-tay) Moderately slow.

andantino (ahn-dahn-TEE-noh) A little faster than *andante.*

anima (AH-nee-mah) Spirit, life, animation.

animato (ah-nee-MAH-toh) Lively, spirited.

arpeggio (are-PED-jee-oh) Rapidly playing the notes of a chord one at a time consecutively, up or down.

a tempo (ah TEHM-poh) Return to the previous tempo.

cantabile (cahn-TAH-bil-lay) Singing style.

chanty (CHAN-tee) Work song sung by sailors, often in rhythm with their work motions.

chord (KORD) Simultaneous sounding of three or more notes.

chromatic (kro-MAH-tik) Series of notes proceeding by half steps.

coda (KOH-dah) Extra musical section at the end of a piece. Often indicated by the symbol: ⊕

con brio (kone BREE-oh) With vigor, spirit, gusto.

con vivo (kone VEE-voh) With life, animation.

cresc. = **crescendo** (cre-SHEN-doh) Gradually increasing in loudness. Also abbreviated: ⎯⎯⎯

damper pedal Piano foot pedal *farthest to the right.* Used to blend sounds and connect notes smoothly. See page 12.

D.C. = **da capo** (dah KAH-poh) Return to the beginning and repeat.

D.C. al fine (ahl FEE-nay) Return to the beginning and repeat, ending at the word *Fine.*

dim. = **diminuendo** (di-min-you-END-oh) Becoming gradually less loud. Also abbreviated: ⎯⎯⎯

dissonance (DISS-uh-nunce) Simultaneous musical sounds that are harsh or unpleasant to the listener.

dolce (DOL-chay) Sweetly, softly.

dynamic marks Same as *expression marks.*

8ᵛᵃ Abbreviation for *octave higher sign.*

energico (eh-NAIR-jee-koh) Energetic, powerful.

espressivo (ehs-preh-SEE-voh) With expression and emotion.

expression marks Signs used to show different levels of loud and soft. For example, *p mf ff*

f = **forte** (FOHR-tay) Loud.

fermata (ferr-MAH-tah) Hold or wait on a note or chord longer than its normal duration. Symbol: ⌢

ff = **fortissimo** (fohr-TISS-ee-moh) Very loud.

fine (FEE-nay) End. (see *D.C. al fine*)

gavotte (gah-VOTT) Lively French dance in 4/4 meter, popular duing 1600's and 1700's. See page 31.

giocoso (jee-oh-KOH-soh) Humorously, playfully.

grazioso (graht-zee-OH-soh) Gracefully.

half step The interval from one key (of the keyboard) to the next closest key, black or white.

hold Name sometimes given to a *fermata*: ⌢

interval Distance in sound between one note and another.

largo (LAHR-goh) Very slow, solemn.

legato (lah-GAH-toh) Notes played in a smooth and connected manner. Usually indicated with a *slur*.

leger line (LED-jer) Short horizontal line used as an extension above or below the staff. Used for writing individual notes beyond the range of the staff.

leggiero (led-jee-AIR-oh) Light, delicate. Abbreviation: *legg.*

lento (LEN-toh) Slow, but not as slow as *largo*.

L.H. Abbreviation of left hand.

maestoso (my-ess-TOH-soh) Majestic, dignified, proudly.

marcato (mahr-CAH-toh) Marked, emphasized.

mazurka (mah-ZUR-kah) Polish folk dance in 3/4 time.

medley (MED-lee) Group of pieces played in succession without interruption as one continuous unit.

meno mosso (MAY-noh MOHS-soh) Less motion, less quickly.

mf = **mezzo forte** (MET-zoh FOHR-tay) Medium loud, softer than *forte*.

metronome (MET-roh-nome) Device to determine tempo in music, measured in beats per minute. See pages 8 and 9.

minor Chord, melody or scale often having a sad, mysterious, or spooky sound.

minuet (min-you-ETT) Dignified dance for couples with slow to moderate 3/4 meter. Originated in France. See page 30.

misterioso (miss-teer-ee-OH-soh) Mysteriously.

M. M. Abbreviation of Maelzel's metronome. See page 9.

moderato (mah-dur-AH-toh) At a moderate tempo.

molto (MOHL-toh) Very, much.

mp = **mezzo piano** (MET-zoh pee-YAH-noh) Medium soft, louder than *piano*.

octave (AHK-tiv) Interval of an 8th. The top and bottom notes have the same letter name.

octave higher sign Play the notes one octave higher than written. Abbreviation: *8va* or *8*. Often used with a dotted line above the notes affected. See page 28.

op. = **opus** (OH-puss) Unit of musical work usually numbered in chronological order. May be a composition of any length, from a short single piece to a full symphony.

opera (AH-per-ah) Musical drama with emphasis on singing. Performed on a theater stage with costumes, scenery etc. with an orchestral accompaniment.

operetta (ah-per-ETT-ah) Short *opera*. The plot is usually not serious.

p = **piano** (pee-YAA-noh) Soft.

pesante (peh-SAHN-teh) Heavy, weighty.

phrase (FRAZE) Group of successive notes dividing a melody or accompaniment pattern into a logical section. This is similar to the way a sentence is divided into sections.

phrase mark Curved line placed over or under groups of notes, indicating the length of a *phrase*. The notes within a phrase are usually played *legato*.

piu mosso (PEE-oo MOHS-soh) More motion, faster.

poco a poco (POH-koh ah POH-koh) Little by little, gradually.

polka (POL-kah) Lively dance for couples using small steps and hops. See page 6.

pp = **pianissimo** (pee-ah-NISS-ee-moh) Very soft.

presto (PRESS-toh) Very fast, faster than *allegro*.

primo (PREE-moh) First part or player. In a piano duet the first part (upper) is labeled *primo*. The second part (lower) is labeled *secondo*.

rall. = **rallentando** (rah-lenn-TAHN-doh) Gradually growing slower in tempo.

repeat sign Two dots in the staff to the left of a double bar indicating that the previous section is to be repeated once.

repertoire (REH-per-twar) Musical compositions previously studied, mastered and currently maintained by a musician or musical group so that performance can be given with a minimum of preparation.

R. H. Abbreviation of right hand.

rit. = **ritardando** (ree-tahr-DAHN-doh) Becoming gradually slower in tempo.

ritard. Another abbreviation for *ritardando*.

root 1) Key note, fundamental note, or tonic note of a chord. Lowest note of a root position chord. 2) First degree of a scale.

scale (SKAIL) Sequence of musical tones collectively forming a key or tonality. Usually named after the starting note.

scherzando (skare-TSAHN-doh) Playfully, jokingly.

scherzo (SKARE-tso) Light, playful or humorous piece of music. *Scherzo* literally means joke.

secondo (seh-KAHN-doh) Second part or player. See *primo*.

semplice (SEMM-plee-chay) Simple, plain.

sfz = **sforzando** (sfor-TSAHN-doh) Sudden emphasis or accent on a note or chord.

slur Curved line placed over or under groups of notes indicating *legato*. Often the same as a *phrase mark*.

spiritoso (spir-ih-TOH-soh) Animated, with spirit.

staccato (stah-KAH-toh) Short, detached, separated. A staccato note is held for slightly less than its normal duration. Indicated with a dot placed above or below a note head.

syncopation (sink-uh-PAY-shun) Rhythmic emphasis of notes OFF the regular numbered counts. See page 32.

tempo di marcia (TEMM-poh dih MAHR-chee-ah) March time.

tempo di valse (TEHM-poh dih VALSZ) Waltz time.

tempo mark Word or words at the beginning of a piece of music explaining the rate of speed at which the music is to be played. For example, *allegro, andante, tempo di marcia*. May also describe a mood expressed as the music is played.

tonic (TAHN-ik) Starting note of a major or minor scale.

transpose (trans-POZE) To play a melody or chord in a different key, starting on a higher or lower note. When transposing, a different key signature, notes from a different scale and a different hand position are used.

triad (TRY-add) Chord with three notes.

vivace (vee-VAH-chay) Lively, quick.

whole step The distance from one key (of the keyboard) to another *with one key in between*. The same as two *half steps*.

48

Reference Page - continued on page 46 - also see Music Dictionary on page 46

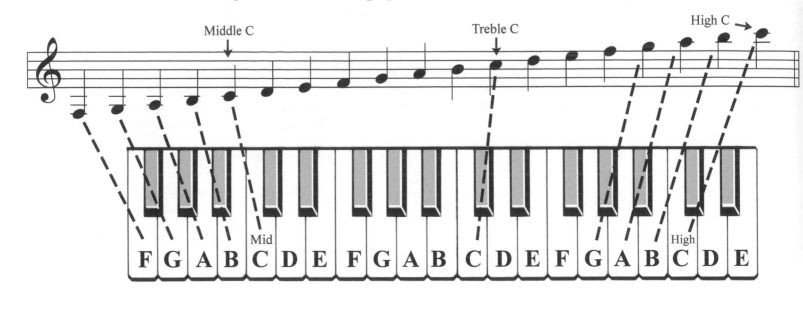

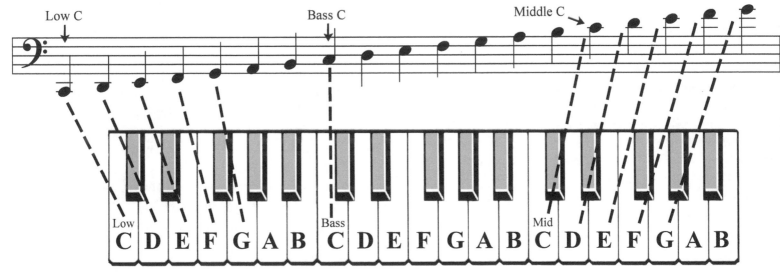

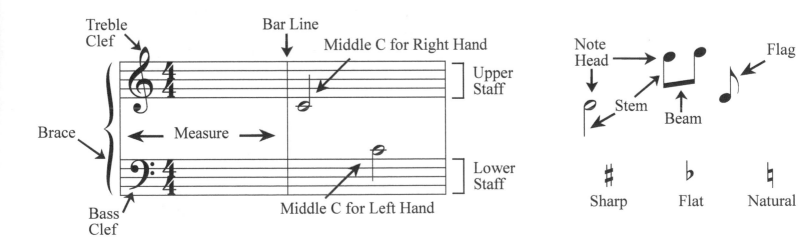

TIME SIGNATURES:

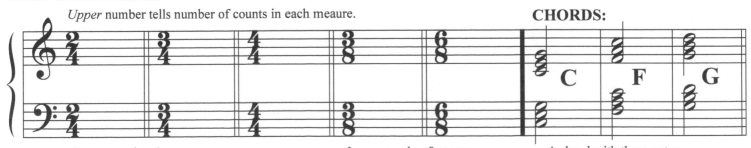

Upper number tells number of counts in each meaure.

CHORDS:

Lower number 4 means **quarter note** gets one count.

Lower number 8 means **eighth note** gets one count.

A chord with three notes is called a *triad* (TRY-add).